Creating Ikebana

Ichiyo School

Akihiro Kasuya

SHUFUNOTOMO/JAPAN PUBLICATIONS

First edition/First printing: February, 2005

© Copyright in Japan 2005 by Akihiro Kasuya
Photographs by Kenichi Ogoshi
Edited by Michiko Kinoshita
Book design by Momoyo Nishimura
English text supervised by Jane Singer

Published by SHUFUNOTOMO CO., LTD.
2-9, Kanda Surugadai, Chiyoda-ku, Tokyo, 101-8911 Japan

Distributed by Japan Publications Trading Co.,Ltd.

Distributors:
United States: Kodansha America, Inc. through Oxford University Press,
198 Madison Avenue, New York, NY 10016, U.S.A.
Canada: Fitzhenry and Whiteside Ltd., 195 Allstate Parkway, Markham, Ontario, L3R 4T8.
Australia and New Zealand: Bookwise International Pty., Ltd. 174 Cormack Road, Wingfield, South Australia 5013, Australia.
Asia and Japan: Japan Publications Trading Co., Ltd., 1-2-1, Sarugaku-cho, Chiyoda-ku, Tokyo 101-0064, Japan.

ISBN-13:978-4-88996-182-9
ISBN-10:4-88996-182-8

Printed in China

Preface

It is my great pleasure to publish this book, "Creating Ikebana," today, twenty-one years after succeeding my father, Meikof Kasuya, in 1983 and becoming the third headmaster, or Iemoto, of the Ichiyo School. In publishing this collection of my works, I selected some representative arrangements from those that I have created over the past two decades. As the arrangements are not organized in chronological order, it may be difficult for the reader to follow the changes in my work over time. However, each arrangement indeed captures my development and state of mind at the time; to me, each work is as clear a reflection of its time as are the popular songs I used to enjoy.

According to Japanese convention, and especially in the traditional ikebana world, the oldest son in a family should succeed to his father's position or profession. Since I was the youngest of four brothers, as a child I never thought that I would enter the ikebana world. Nevertheless, I always enjoyed playing with the leftover flowers and other ikebana materials after ikebana classes and I was pleased when my father or the other teachers encouraged me by praising my arrangements. At the time, arranging flowers was a form of play for me, and, more than my brothers, I enjoyed visiting the ikebana classrooms as a boy to watch the students learning ikebana and the teachers applying their skills in arranging. In my late teens, with my older brothers all taking up other professions, I found myself left as the only one to succeed to my father's work.

Although ikebana was thus always a part of my life and I naturally came to remember the names of the materials often used in arrangements, it was only when I reached my twenties that I began to study the art seriously. After that came many years of inner turmoil, as I asked myself whether I liked ikebana enough to make it my life's work. In the end, I decided that whether I really liked ikebana or not was not an easy question to answer and really not that important; even among ikebana materials, there are some that are inspiring and others that aren't. I found that this unpredictable encounter with materials was one of the greatest sources of pleasure for me in my ikebana practice.

Every material has its own characteristics and essential nature. This is as true with ikebana as it is with cooking, where the use of fresh, high-quality ingredients practically guarantees delicious dishes, yet a skillful cook can bring out the best flavors from even the most ordinary ingredients. When I select an ikebana material I first try to discern its essential features in a process that is akin to communicating with the flowers. This encounter with the materials, even more than arranging them, is one of the most charming and enjoyable aspects of ikebana.

Ikebana has always been an indispensable part of my life and the focus of many years of hard work and dedication. I hope that through reading this book you will also come to appreciate the pleasures of this art form.

Finally, I would like to thank everyone involved in creating this book: my staff; Ichiyo School members around the world; my family, of course; and the Shufunotomo Publishing Company.

Akihiro Kasuya

Contents

The Beauty of Lines

In ikebana the main branch, or *yakueda*, is also called a line material, which means that linear movement is one of the most significant considerations when composing an arrangement. There are all kinds of branches, each with its own line, and it is impossible to find two of exactly the same kind of branch with the same linear movement, even with the same material. Each composition will differ from others according to how you observe line materials and how you express their characters in your arrangements. That is one factor behind the great appeal of ikebana.

Page 1: Bulrush and sunflower in containers designed by the Iemoto
Pages 2–3: Weeping willow in white "crater" containers designed by the Iemoto
Page 4: Herbaceous peony and white alder in ceramic containers by Meikof Kasuya
Page 6: Tulip and yellow-band lily in containers designed by the Iemoto
Page 8: Reeves spirea, lily, sweet pea and green pea in white containers designed by the Iemoto
Pages 98-99: Photographs from magazine "*Fujingaho*" by permission of Hachette Fujingaho

Allium and peony in a modified vase and plated glass container

A plated glass container with loops through which stems can pass has been placed atop a unique, well-balanced vase that looks like three balls perched naturalistically one upon the other. It's a pleasure to work with the interesting natural linear movement of allium stems, which are inserted through the loops and twisted together. An accent of peonies was added to emphasize the lively curvature of the allium stems.

Allium and peony in a modified vase and plated glass container

I secured the alliums as shown by twining the stems around the handle-like blue glass loops attached to the bottom of the basin. Manipulation during their growth period forces the allium stems into twisting curves. I stood them upright to add a lively, light-hearted touch to this composition. Finally I added an accent by arranging the two straight-stemmed allium, with their large, ball-like flowers and vertical lines.

Tulip, fennel, sword fern and kiwi vine in an oblong ceramic container

First I inserted kiwi vines one by one, carefully twining and twisting each vine to make the most of their delicate, naturally curving lines. I then arranged the other materials to complement the vines, in the order of fennel, sword fern and tulip.

Tulip and kiwi vine in a Philippine hollowed wooden bowl with a handle and a round ceramic bowl

Kiwi vines that were roughly woven together to resemble a fragile basket were placed in the wooden bowl as shown, then a large round ceramic bowl was added to anchor the vines. Tulips were inserted separately in stable positions. This lovely arrangement produces an unexpected harmony.

Lily and aloe in a container made by the Iemoto

    I crossed the sharp spear-like aloe leaves at the mouth of the vase, and inserted a vertical branch of graceful lily for a contrastingly soft impression. The resulting combination of their two different characters achieves a lively and vivid composition.

Two kinds of tulips in a modified vase made by the Iemoto

I have always felt attracted by the elasticity of tulip stems, which sometimes seem to be strong but are actually fragile and at other times seem fragile but are actually strong. The distinctive feature of tulips is their tendency to gradually change the direction of their stems as they grow. It is pleasant to see how these tulips gradually change their linear movement. The visual unity of the material and the container creates powerful energy in this work.

Aspidistra, limonium and small chrysanthemum in an oblong container
    The curve of an aspidistra leaf will be softened if you artificially tear it lengthwise, as shown, but leave the tip whole. Although this technique has been widely accepted in ikebana for decades, it is still one of my favorite ways to treat materials.

Great cat-tail and clematis in a vase made by the Iemoto
Great cat-tail grasses break easily, so they should be arranged with care and not bent too far.
I feel myself expressing the character of great cat-tail grasses best when curling them
gently into large graceful arcs.

Japanese Rikyubai (pear bush; *Exochorda racemosa*) and freesia in a modified tall vase made by the Iemoto

Freesia is entwined around a pear bush branch. My intention with this arrangement was to create linear movement that combines straight lines and spreading lines that branch off from the straight line like the fingers of a widely spread hand. The vase can't stand alone, but it stands here because I have achieved a balance with the materials.

Silver wattle and anemone in a two-legged container made by the Iemoto
When we remove all the leaves from the silver wattle, its yellow florets and gently waving stem lines remind us of a gentle spring breeze. As a finishing touch, the vividly colored anemone provides a visual contrast.

Narcissus and paper filaments in paired flower containers designed by the Iemoto
  The flowers and narcissus leaves seem to playing tug-of-war from their separate containers. The many thread-like lines of polygonum filiforme play an important role in highlighting the bridging horizontal lines in this composition.

Weeping willow, spindle tree and tulip in a basin designed by the Iemoto
  This creative work was simply composed of three different kinds of lines — the broadly arching lines of a willow branch, the dynamic straight lines of a spindle tree branch and the gentle curvature of a tulip stem. Only one stem or branch of each material was used, and all three were placed close together. The attention-getting spindle tree was arranged upside down.

Hime-basho (*Musa coccinea*) leaf, pine, *Strelitzia augusta* and tara vine in a vase made by the Iemoto

Using just three materials — Hime-basho leaves, pine, and *Strelitzia augusta* — would have created quite an adequate composition. However, when I added the small tara vines with their wild and intriguing curves, the work became much more attractive.

Anthurium, eucalyptus and tortuosa weeping willow in a basin made by the Iemoto

The gently curved lines of the eucalyptus and the elegant lines of the tortuosa weeping willow extend in opposite directions and intersect with each other so that character of each is revealed more distinctly.

Calla lily in a ceramic pot

    The remarkable interwoven lines of the calla lily impart a vivid impression. Their strong, aesthetically pleasing curvature shows off their delightful elasticity, which they almost seem to take pride in. If the calla stems are too straight they will lack elastic movement, while if the arranger tries too hard to force the stems to curve they can easily break.

Glass Containers

You will find that there are many different types, designs, and textures of glass containers. Some containers are transparent or colored-transparent, while others are semi-transparent or opaque. Popular glass containers include plates, basins, deep bowls, pots, cylindrical or square containers, angular containers, and irregular-shaped containers. Because most glass is transparent, the water and floral material inside the container can be seen. This factor must be considered when you create your arrangement.

Lily and Japanese fatsia in glass containers

Here I arranged the fatsia leaves so they would rest at the base of the two containers, then inserted the fatsia stems into one of the containers. Because the fatsia stems are firm but elastic, they can support the lilies inside the container. The finished arrangement looks very attractive, providing an intriguing contrast between the large and robust leaves and the beauty of the stem lines inside the wave-shaped containers.

Lily and anthurium in a glass container

In this work lilies were inserted into the diagonal opening at the top of this globe-shaped frosted glass container in a stable, stationery position. I added anthurium for balance and support.

Cat-tail and rocks in a rectangular glass container

In this composition I placed a rock strategically beneath the container and filled the container with water. The cat-tails and rocks were arranged inside the container to look as though the cat-tails were growing from the rocks. This naturalistic effect imparts a feeling of softness to the arrangement.

Hidden lily (*Curucuma*), iris leaves and stones in a glass vase

Here I put a few large, irregularly shaped stones in a glass container and arranged some hidden lilies around them. You must take care to avoid scratching glass containers when you arrange with rocks.

Anthurium and sansevieria in bean-shaped containers

This arrangement uses two bean-shaped glass containers with openings in the middle. The mouth of the top container opens to the side and the mouth of the bottom container opens on top. I have put sufficient water inside the lower container and arranged sansevieria in it so that it appears to be reflected in the surface of the water. Another sansevieria leaf was placed facing upwards to create the feeling of curving movement. Because sansevieria is a strong material, I also arranged a long-limbed anthurium to punctuate the space, as if someone is taking a breath.

Camellia in a glass container
    Camellia has been inserted through the openings of a cylindrical container.

Hydrangea and rabbit-ear iris leaves in a glass vase

I like to arrange hydrangea in glass containers. In this arrangement I placed the hydrangea at left and right facing away from each other, with the rabbit-ear iris leaves extending upwards in the middle. The finished arrangement appears to me to resemble hands raised in glee.

Boston fern and craspedia in glass containers

Two colored glass containers were set one on top of the other, with a ball-shaped container on the top and a container with a wave-shaped mouth at the base. I arranged craspedias and ferns in the space between the containers. When you curl ferns around each other you must take care not to break their delicate stems. The massed craspedias provide a lovely picture here, looking like moons revolving around the glass ball.

Sandersonia (Christmas bells) and tara vine in a glass container
 Tara vines have been intertwined to form a round, cylindrical shape. Sandersonia has been woven among the vines. To me they resemble massed players in a rugby scrummage.

Delphinium and tortuosa weeping willow in a glass bowl
Vines of tortuosa weeping willow were coiled together and placed vertically in a deep glass container. I then arranged clusters of delphinium among the vines to create line and movement and to present a beautiful contrast with the massed weeping willow.

Allium and glass ball in a cylindrical glass container
Compositions like this one, which features allium arranged inside and emerging from a glass container, have a mysterious ambiance.

Kousa dogwood and glass ball in a glass container

 Kousa dogwood branches extend straight up, and their flowers and leaves face upward like an open palm. Here I have placed a single branch to span the container and the glass ball. The lively curved branch provides a dynamic, jovial impression, with its colorful flowers blooming in every direction.

Eucalyptus and tulip in a glass vase
 The tulips in the picture are showing us new faces as they bloom. It is interesting to observe the process of tulips gradually opening their blossoms over time.

Calla lily and asparagus myriocladus in a glass vase

Here, calla lilies were entwined together to make rounded arcs. If one of the stems happens to break or fall, the completed spherical shape of the composition will immediately be lost. Each stem must be balanced perfectly with the others to form this rounded outline and to provide tension within the composition.

Butterfly orchid, sweet pea and Japanese bird's nest fern in a glass container
I arranged the bird's nest leaves to emphasize the contrasting colors of their emerald green surfaces and pale undersides. White butterfly orchids and pink sweet peas were added to harmonize with the other components.

Sunflower and bulbinella in a glass vase
This composition nicely combines two dynamic materials, bulbinella and sunflowers.

Hydrangea and Japanese iris leaves in a glass container
The shape of the iris leaves reminds me of animal horns.

Lace cap hydrangea in a glass container
Here I have arranged clusters of hydrangea in a glass container. The inside surface of this container is rough and irregular, while the outside is smooth.

Calla lily and monstera in a glass container
In ikebana arrangements, floral material is not supposed to touch the container or the floor. However, I wanted to challenge this convention and allow the leaves to touch the floor to emphasize the bold character and strength of the material in the composition.

Golden calla lily, peegee hydrangea and monstera leaves in a glass container
I arranged monstera leaves and calla lilies together to support each other at one end of the container. Peegee hydrangea were then added for a softening effect.

Hydrangea and allium in a glass container

I have combined hydrangea with allium in this composition. The artificially curved lines of the allium stems impart a strong impression in combination with the hydrangea. I arranged the flowers so that their stems inside the water would be hidden.

Bamboo

The thick-stemmed Mosochiku bamboo (*Phyllostachys pubescens*) is one of my favorite materials, frequently appearing in my arrangements. The reason is that it has thicker, more succulent stalks and stronger joints than the common Japanese Madake bamboo (*Phyllostachys bambusoides*), so the Mosochiku bamboo imparts an extremely robust impression.

In Japan it is said that bamboo trees bring good luck to people because of their amazingly rapid and vigorous growth. Furthermore, the spaces between the joints of a bamboo stalk have been regarded as something mysterious, possessing an enigmatic force.

In ikebana we strive to respect not only the nature of floral materials but their life force. When I use a bamboo tube as a container or perforate a bamboo stalk with holes for inserting flower stems, I can sense that some kind of sacred spirit is dwelling within the bamboo itself. This is true of flowers as well: When I work with flowers and *washi*, or Japanese paper, I am also aware of a mysterious spirit residing within the flower.

Lily in a green bamboo tube
The lily stem has been inserted through holes in a bamboo tube.

Tulip in a bamboo tube, yellow glass vase

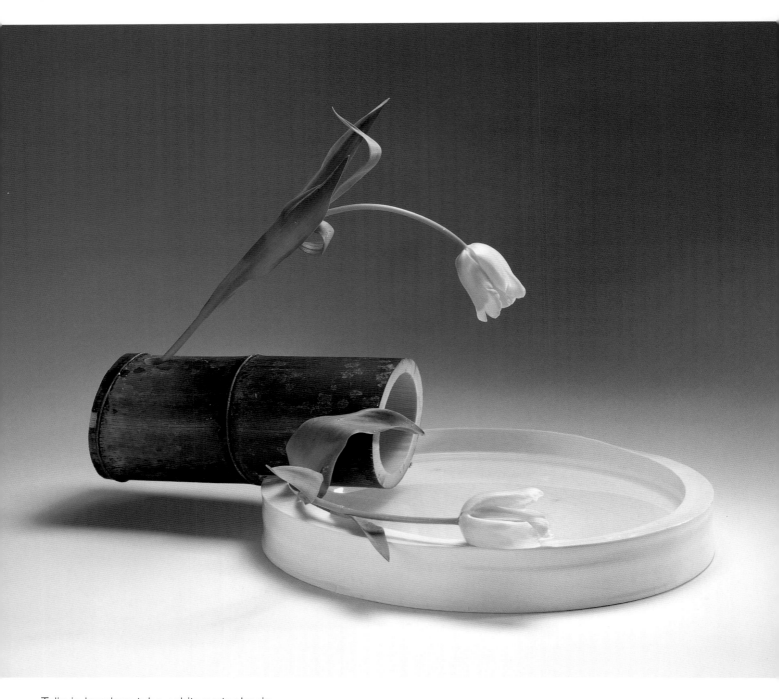

Tulip in bamboo tube, white water basin

King protea in a green bamboo tube, white water basin
   The King protea stems are stabilized by the weight of a bamboo tube in an exquisite balance.

Banana leaf, Casablanca lily and a woven sheet of bamboo in a ceramic basin
Casablanca lilies and a sheet of woven bamboo have been rolled up in a fresh green banana leaf.

Aspidistra lily in a green bamboo tube
A bamboo tube acts as a paperweight when it is placed atop an aspidistra, with its elegant curving lines.

Hibiscus and a green bamboo tube atop a ceramic bowl
This hibiscus is the very picture of tranquility.

Hibiscus, Japanese fatsia and a green bamboo tube atop a ceramic bowl
Hibiscus blossoms, placed together with the Japanese fatsia, add a playful air to this composition.

Japanese apricot, tulip and green bamboo tubes in a ceramic basin

A curving branch of flowering Japanese apricot and three drooping tulip stems, each set in holes in bamboo tubes at opposite ends of a basin, form appealing intersecting lines, like two ends of a connecting bridge.

Two kinds of nandina and a green bamboo tube, glass vase
The lower and higher masses of tinted nandina berries create an unexpected harmony.

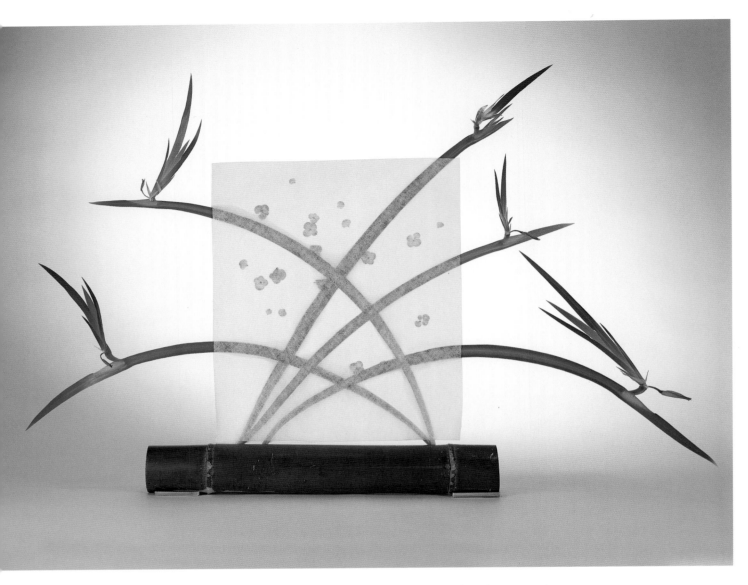

American fringed iris and *washi* paper with dried hydrangea petals, green bamboo container

In this artistic composition, spear-like arched stems of American fringed iris extend to both sides from the bamboo container. In front and behind the iris are sheets of Japanese paper which contain scattered petals of dried hydrangea.

Tulip, *washi* paper with pine needles covering a thin strip of bamboo, glass vase

This impressive and unusual work features a drum made of a bamboo ring covered by Japanese paper decorated with pine needles. A low-bowing tulip serves as a drumstick.

White and red flowering quince and chrysanthemum in a tall bamboo basket, stone container

By covering the stone container with a bamboo basket, two different spaces are formed, both inside and outside the basket. To dispel the cramped impression that could be caused by confining the materials inside the basket, we arrange the flowering quince and chrysanthemum from the outside by inserting them through the weave of the basket. Thus the basket plays an important role in this arrangement.

Sunflower, fruit-laden quince and delphinium in a Philippine bamboo totebag
This totebag hung on a cloth-covered branch resembles a bird nest.

Japanese catalpa, gentian, *Viburnum dilatatum* and small chrysanthemum in a bamboo basket with a pot

It is said that the combination of a bamboo basket and autumn flowers and grasses makes for quintessential ikebana arrangements. In this work, I have arranged more materials than would typically be used to convey a sense of the latter days of autumn.

Shiratama camellia and gentian in a bamboo basket with a lid
The lid of the basket, stood vertically between two camellia branches, becomes an integral element in this composition.

Azalea and plantain lily leaves in a bamboo vase of thick-stemmed Mosochiku bamboo (*Phyllostachys pubescens*)

The thick-stemmed Mosochiku bamboo vase itself is a focus of this arrangement. This rough-edged container, which has been chopped with a hatchet, conveys an energetic, vigorous air. The exuberant plantain lily leaves achieve a favorable balance with the vase.

Anthurium, palm and Japanese bird's nest fern in a bamboo basket

This bamboo basket is a type that is usually used for agricultural work, and can serve as a stool for farmers. It can be bent in any direction but will rarely fall. The materials are arranged freely facing varying directions and curving around the basket in order to strongly express different types of movement.

Japanese bird's nest fern, starwort, elegant lily and tara vine in a bamboo basket

In this dramatic composition, the dynamic lines of the bird's nest fern remind us of a tangle of seaweed floating in the water. The leaves are arranged in streamlined fashion all facing the same direction in order to evoke the image of plants spreading out in the sea. The starwort and elegant lilies, on the other hand, look more like schools of fish swimming together.

In Various Containers

For ikebana the container plays several roles: It is not only for holding the materials and the water, but it also functions as a significant element in an arrangement. Its form, color, appearance and relationship with water become important aspects of the composition as a whole.

While every plant on earth is produced and receives its life force from nature, every ikebana container is the product of its creator's creativity, raw materials like porcelain clay and glaze, and the appropriate temperature of the fire in the kiln.

Ikebana combines all of these elements. It results from the arranger's inspiration and emotions, which arise from the combination of materials, container and space.

Long-needled pine and camellia in an oblong ceramic container
These camellia twigs, cut longer than the length of the container, look as tightly coiled as springs.
They add a sharp edge to the linear movement of the camellia branches.

Flowering quince and fennel in an original white vase designed by Yukio Nakagawa
Flowering quince is secured by bracing its lateral branches against the sides of the container.
The upward-facing movement of both the container and the branches brings out a nice
harmony. The strong fennel branches are arranged with their ends braced against
the container's walls on opposite sides to secure the arrangement.

Winter sweet and common daffodil in a white oblong ceramic basin

In this composition I tried to express the dense solidity of the winter sweet tree. To do that, I laid one long, thick branch of winter sweet extending to the right edge of the basin and another, thinner branch with a parallel extension under the water. I made sure that sufficient space on the water's surface was left uncovered by the materials.

Winter sweet and freesia in an original ceramic container designed by the Iemoto

. In this arrangement, my intention was to create a relaxing, expansive atmosphere by having branches of winter sweet extend outward at both sides.

Magnolia and yellow-band lily in a white three-legged vase
    The attractive sensuous curve of this vase resulted naturally from the intense heat of the kiln when the vase was baked. The vase seems to be telling me, "Arrange a branch so that it complements this curve."

Magnolia in four original vases designed by the Iemoto
    These four wide-bottomed ceramic vases are assiduously stacked atop each other, with each vase shifted slightly to the left of the one below it, in order to produce a perfect balance with the single branch of flowering magnolia branch inserted at the top. The magnolia is inserted with care to lean to the opposite, right side of the top vase.

Cymbidium orchid and large stone in an original modified container made by the Iemoto

This container gives us a powerful impression once a stone has been placed inside it. Two lovely orchid stems are inserted in the narrow spaces between the container and the stone. The orchid blossoms resemble gracefully fluttering butterflies.

Orchid and cyclamen in a white modified container with multiple mouths
The exuberant orchid roots express their vigor and natural energy when they are placed in this uniquely shaped container. Lovely cyclamen flowers lend a colorful yet softening air to the composition.

Japanese fatia and Casablanca lily in original ceramic containers designed by the Iemoto
Casablanca lilies, delicately fragrant and absolutely beautiful in appearance, are among my favorite flowers. In this work, all the petals have been removed from the Casablanca lily so that only the stamens and pistils remain, allowing them to show their attractive forms.

Hydrangea, veronica and iris leaf in a ceramic bowl
The two erect stems of veronica with their flower spikes look full of life, while the other veronica leaves, with their arching lines, seem to be putting on airs and graces.

Yellow-band iris and small rocks in a modified container made by Ryoji Koie

This container has a shallow depression for water where I secured the yellow-band iris with small stones. With this composition my intention was actually to acknowledge the remarkable resilience and vitality of the leaves pinned down by rocks.

Two kinds of calla lily in original rectangular containers designed by the Iemoto
  Calla lilies are arranged in three rectangular containers so that their stems cross each other at different angles. The thick stems and the two contrasting colors of flowers produce a highly pleasing visual impression.

Lotus in original containers designed by the Iemoto

These lotus leaves of different sizes, arranged in containers I made especially for this arrangement, display varied and fascinating surfaces and graceful movement. The work has a rhythmic, expansive atmosphere. I may have conceived of this composition, but I think that the lotus themselves arranged it.

Rose, green calla lily and smoke tree in an original ceramic container designed by the Iemoto

This simple white container was chosen to complement the two roses, with their naturally curving stems, and the dramatic curve of the green calla lily leaves.

Anthurium and yellow jasmine in an original modified vase made by the Iemoto

Anthurium flowers show interesting movement, but they require a high level of skill and technique by the arranger. In this work, the delicate lines of the yellow jasmine branches contrast vividly with the shorter but bolder lines of the anthurium.

Cockscomb, patrinia and Japanese miscanthus in a ceramic bowl made by Ryoji Koie

A large, robust cluster of cockscomb is arranged on the right side of this round white container, and patrinia is loosely massed on the left side. Finally, Japanese miscanthus is added to unify the arrangement and add harmony.

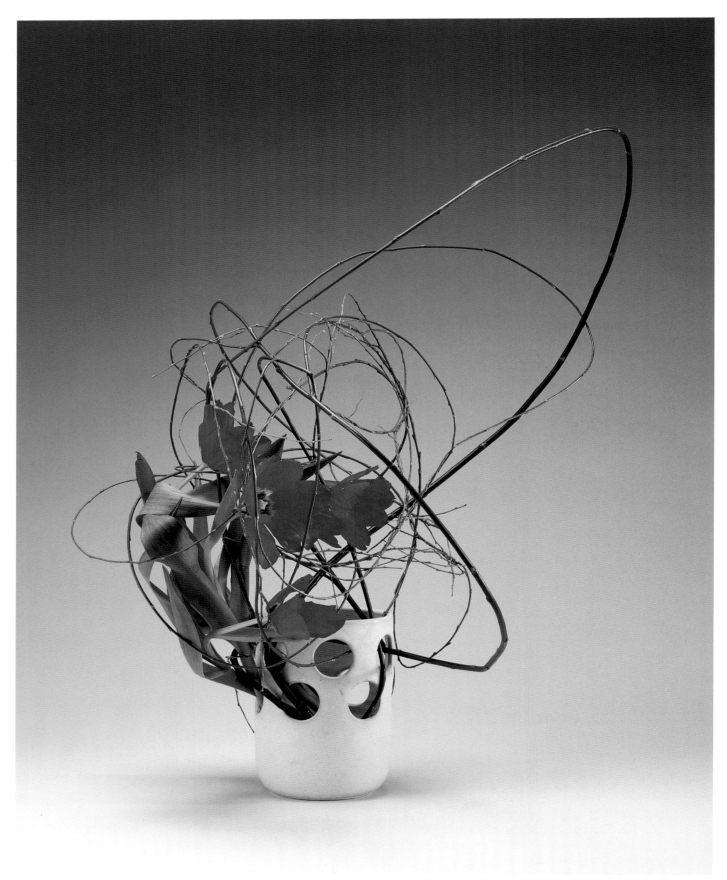

Tulip in an original square black container made by Taiji Tomimoto

This container, cut into a box shape, suggests to me the image of a slab of rich earth. Tulips harmonize nicely with the container, and with their lively expressiveness and movement, they seem to me to be carrying on a dialogue with the earth below them.

Tulip and weeping willow in an original white vase designed by Meikof Kasuya

Sweeping loops of weeping willow branches, inserted repeatedly through the holes on the side of the vase, have found an ideal partner in these richly colored flowering tulips, which are playfully enclosed within the loops.

Tree peony and ornamental cabbage in an original black container made by Masahiro Shimizu
This black boat-shaped container is strong enough to stand up to the floral materials: the magnificent tree peony and the ornamental cabbage. This is a dramatic and artistic work that brings out the best of the individual character of each material so that even the petals of the peony attract our attention.

Cyclamen, orchid leaf and Kanchiku bamboo in an original black container made by Masahiro Shimizu
This uniquely shaped container has a long, narrow mouth on its sloping upper surface and on its right side. The elegant, curving line of a pliable Kanchiku bamboo stalk emerges from the side mouth, while cyclamen and an orchid leaf are inserted in the upper surface mouth. To me this lovely work suggests an image of fishing for cyclamen flowers with a fishing rod of Kanchiku bamboo.

Herbaceous peony and wisteria branch in a glazed vase

When all the leaves are removed from the wisteria branches, they reveal pale green branches with delicate straight lines. This work successfully combines mass, with the brilliantly hued peony flowers, and the soft lines of the willow branch.

Camellia, sweet pea and wisteria in an original tall vase

To bring out the attractive character of wisteria vines, one very long vine, arching gracefully, is arranged in an upright position. Sweet peas and a camellia flower serve as complements to emphasize the elegant curvature of the wisteria.

Calla lily and areca palm (*Chrysalidocarpus lutescens*) in a deep ceramic bowl

    Here I have arranged the calla lilies to extend in varied directions, then set the outsized areca palm leaves, with their gently curving lines, in the space among the calla lilies.

Dendrobium phalaenopsis, sandersonia, heliconia and *Aspidistra elatior* in two stone-shaped ceramic vases

Aspidistra leaves are traditionally used to wrap Japanese sushi. In this composition, aspidistra performs dynamically as a dramatic accent, laid beneath the vases or arranged like wings or flags in the wind. The other floral materials are arranged freely and naturally.

Japanese catalpa, sansevieria and sunflower in a tall line-patterned vase
      These long, drooping Japanese catalpa leaves have the appearance of a bird's unfolding wings. The arrangement seems to be about to fly away.

Sunflower and caladium in an original black box-shaped container made by Yasuji Tomimoto

   This creative hexagonal container has a shallow hollow scooped out of its upper face for holding water. The small ceramic piece with a number of small holes, which resembles a half-opened tin can lid or a shovelful of earth turned over, is in fact made from the clay scooped out of the hollow. The sunflowers and caladium exhibit a sense of coiled movement, as if they may pop out from the lid at any moment.

Anthurium in a narrow-mouthed vase

The faces of anthurium are so lustrous that you could be excused for assuming these are artificial flowers. However, if you look closely, you can see that each has a different face and expression. In this work I have sought to bring out the dramatic contrast between the face and the underside of the material.

Anthurium and taro leaves in a black pot

This composition is an exciting combination of large-leafed taro and similarly shaped anthurium. The subtle difference between the two materials and their prominent character are well-displayed here.

Cosmos and sword fern in a white vase

The lively movement of the sword fern fronds reminds us of autumn's bracing winds; therefore, I arranged these lovely cosmos flowers as though they were swaying before the fern's gusty breezes. The composition as a whole is representative of the cool crisp days of autumn.

Ikebana in Daily Life

Ikebana arrangements were traditionally displayed in a special alcove in a tatami-floored room called a *tokonoma*. However, ikebana has undergone major changes with the times as Japan has modernized dramatically and our way of life has become more westernized. Today, we arrange ikebana not only in the *tokonoma* but anywhere we wish. This is not surprising: In every age, ikebana has adapted to and reflected people's lifestyles.

In the Ichiyo School, we have always tried to keep our ikebana practice closely related to people's daily lives, and this can be seen in the locations chosen for the arrangements. On the other hand, I think that often the materials or arrangements seem to themselves spontaneously suggest the best place to be displayed.

On the windowsill
Two kinds of tulips, silver wattle and Reeves spirea in original containers designed by the Iemoto

On the sunshine-dappled floor
Tulip in a tall white vase

On a sideboard surface
Japanese iris in an original gourd-shaped container designed by Meikof Kasuya

In the entryway
Rabbit-ear iris and fishing tackle in an original white porcelain bowl by Masamichi Yoshikawa

The centerpiece of a dining room table
   Glory lily, tortuosa weeping willow, *Statice perezii*, smailax asparagus, gentian, Mizuhiki knotgrass (*Polygonum filiforme*) and celosia in original containers designed by the Iemoto

On the floor in a dining area
Fruit-laden quince, cosmos, Janome pine, small chrysanthemum and Mizuhiki knotgrass in a large bowl

Atop a sideboard
  Bottle-brush and clematis in an original round water basin designed by the Iemoto

Ikebana on Exhibition

Ikebana practitioners can exhibit their works in a variety of ways:

(1) In conjunction with other arrangers at a joint exhibition in an exhibition hall.
(2) At a solo exhibition of one large installation or several of the arranger's works in an exhibition hall.
(3) At an open-air ikebana exhibition.
(4) At a show by a single arranger or a joint show with several arrangers at a particular location such as the entrance hall of a public building, a theater hall or foyer, a department store display window or other large public site.
(5) At other kinds of displays.

There is no precise requirement for what ikebana at an exhibition should look like, but most people would agree that the major objective of most exhibitions is to display as wide a variety of arrangements and styles to as many people as possible.

I always try to capture the true expressions or character of the materials and to articulate my thoughts and feelings about them so that I can express this in my arrangements.

Ikebana Today exhibition at Seibu Department Store, Ikebukuro, Tokyo 1986

F's Group Exhibition, 1998

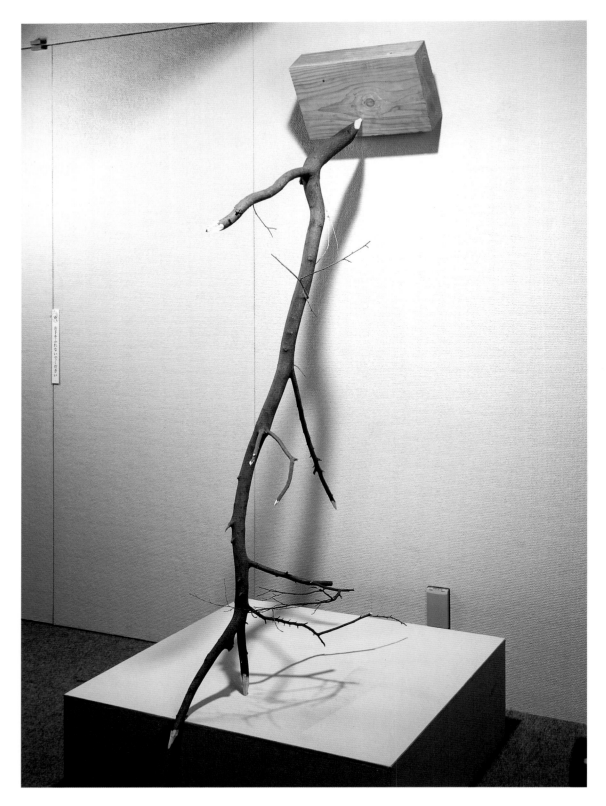

Ikebana Today exhibition at Seibu Department Store, Ikebukuro, Tokyo 1985

Ikebana Today exhibition at Seibu Department Store, Ikebukuro, Tokyo 1984

At Seibu Department Store, Oizumi, Tokyo 1983

At Seibu Department Store, Oizumi, Tokyo 1983

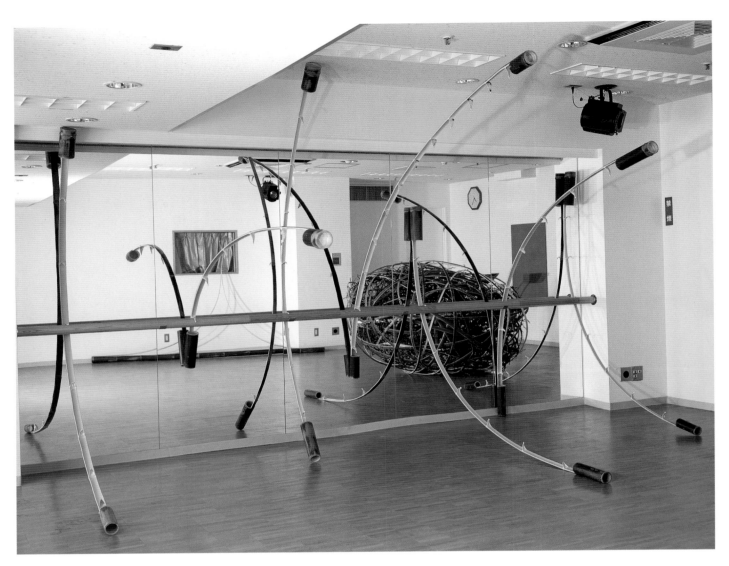

Solo exhibition at a department store in Hachioji, Tokyo 1986

114

115

Open-air Ikebana Exhibition at Showa Memorial Park, Tachikawa, Tokyo 1993

Photo: courtesy of Ikebana International

Open-air Ikebana Exhibition at Hibiya
Park, Tokyo 1995

Photo: courtesy of Ikebana International

In the foyer of Casals Hall, Tokyo 1990

The Japan Ikebana Art Society Exhibition, Tokyo 1990

Demonstration at the Eighth Ikebana International World Convention at the Yokohama Pacifico auditorium, Yokohama, Kanagawa Prefecture 2001

Photo : courtesy of Ikebana International

An ikebana demonstration in winter at a seminar of
the Ichiyo School, Tokyo 2003

Japan Ikebana Association Exhibition at Matsuya Department
Store, Ginza, Tokyo 2003

An ikebana exhibition with potter
Yasuo Yamamoto in Aoyama,
Tokyo 2002

Biography

1947   Born in Tokyo as the third son of Meikoh Kasuya, the second headmaster of the Ichiyo School

1966   Exhibited at the SIS Group Exhibition

1967-70   Studied in the U.S.

1973   Named as acting headmaster
First year of participation in "The Exhibition of the 100 Greatest Ikebana Artists." Began participating actively in exhibitions and events nationwide

1980   Exhibition at Modern Ikebana Art Gallery 1980

1981   Exhibition at Ikebana EXPO Toyota, Japan

1982   Lectures and workshops in U.S. and Europe

1983   Became third Iemoto (headmaster) of the Ichiyo School
Exhibition at Niigata Setsugen Event, Japan

1984   Lectures and workshops in Netherlands, Germany and Switzerland

1985   Lectures and workshops in South Africa, U.K., Taiwan and Karachi (Pakistan)

1986   Demonstration at 5th Ikebana International World Convention in Kyoto, Japan

1987   Lectures and workshops in Taiwan and Thailand
Lectures and workshops in U.S. (San Diego, Peoria, Minneapolis, Tacoma, Dallas, Cleveland, Pittsburgh, Stone Lantern), Jamaica and Argentina

1988   Lectures and workshops in London, Basel (Switzerland), Wiesbaden (Germany) and Castillon du Gard (France).

1989   Lectures and workshop in Hong Kong

1990   Lectures and workshops in Australia and New Zealand
Lectures and workshops in U.K. and U.S. (Tennessee and Washington, D.C.)

1991   Demonstration at 6th Ikebana International World Convention at NHK Hall, Tokyo
Publication of English and Japanese editions of Ikebana book "Ikebana Ichiyo—Hanahazama"

1992   Lectures and workshops in U.S. (Sweetwater and Milwaukee), London, Copenhagen and Basel and Geneva (Switzerland)
Lectures and workshops in U.S.(Colorado Springs, Seattle, Tacoma)

1993   Lectures and workshops in U.S. (Washington, D.C., Florida, Pittsburgh, San Diego, Dallas and Cleveland)
Open-air Ikebana exhibition at Showa Park, Tokyo 1994
Lectures and workshops in U.S. (San Antonio, Sweetwater)
Display and demonstration at New York Metropolitan Museum, U.S.

1995   Demonstration and workshop at the Ikebana International North American Regional Convention in Honolulu, U.S.
Demonstration and workshop at the Ikebana International European Regional Convention in Nîmes, France
Open-air ikebana exhibition at Hibiya Park, Tokyo

1996   Demonstrations in Atlanta and New Jersey, (U.S.)
Lectures and demonstration in Hong Kong
Demonstration and workshop at 7th Ikebana International World Convention at the Nagoya International Convention Hall, Japan

1997   Demonstration and workshop in Atlanta, U.S.

1998   Demonstrations and workshops in U.S. (Florida, New York, Pittsburgh)
Solo exhibition in Soho, New York
Demonstration and workshop in Melbourne, Australia
Demonstration and workshop at 4th Ikebana International South African Regional Symposium in Johannesburg, South Africa

1999   Demonstration at the Japanese Embassy in Cairo, Egypt
Demonstrations in Florida, New York and San Francisco, U.S.
Workshop in Monterey, U.S.
Display at the New York Metropolitan Museum of Art
Demonstration at the Franco-Japanese Institute in Paris

2000   Demonstration and workshop at Ikebana International Australia-New Zealand Regional Convention in Sydney, Australia
Demonstration in Tasmania, Australia
Demonstration, lecture and television appearance in Costa Rica by request of Japanese Embassy
Demonstration and workshop in New Mexico, U.S.
Demonstration, lecture, exhibition and television appearance in Guatemala at request of Japanese Embassy to celebrate inauguration of new president
Total of 3,750 participants in demonstrations and workshops in U.S. (Washington, D.C., Florida, New Orleans)

2001   Exhibition to celebrate 65th anniversary of Ichiyo School at Shin Yokohama New City Hall
Demonstration at 8th Ikebana International World Convention at Pacifico Yokohama Conference Center, Japan
Appearance on NHK TV, BS channel-Ikebana Arrangement
Lectures and workshops in U.S. (Atlanta and Pittsburgh) and U.K.

2002   Lectures and workshops in U.S. and U.K.
Demonstration in New Delhi, 50th anniversary of Japan-India Diplomatic Relations

2003   Lectures and Demonstrations in U.S. and U.K.
Lectures and Demonstrations in Myanmar and Malaysia, by the request of the Ministry of Foreign Affairs
Lectures and workshops in Africa (Algeria and Kenya)
The Ichiyo Symposium in Holland–Demonstration, workshop and exhibition

2004   Demonstrations and workshops in Algeria, Sudan and Bahrain, by invitation of the Japanese Embassies
Lecture and Demonstration for Ikebana International in New York
Lecture and Demonstration in Atlanta, U.S.